MW01452203

Know Jesus: The Gospel According to Mark Bible Study Journal
© 2022 Pillar Church of Washington DC

No part of this publication may be reproduced, stored in a retrieval system, or transmitted in any form or by any means — electronic, mechanical, photocopy, recording, or any other—except for brief quotations in printed reviews, without the prior permission of the publisher.

Scripture quotations have been taken from the Christian Standard Bible®, Copyright © 2017 by Holman Bible Publishers. Used by permission. Christian Standard Bible® and CSB® are federally registered trademarks of Holman Bible Publishers.

KNOW JESUS

The Gospel According to Mark

PillarDC.com

CONTENTS

Introduction	6
1. Mark 1:1–13	10
2. Mark 1:14–28	12
3. Mark 2:1–17	14
4. Mark 4:35–41	16
5. Mark 6:30–44	18
6. Mark 6:45–56	20
7. Mark 7:1–15	22
8. Mark 8:27–38	24
9. Mark 10:17–31	26
10. Mark 10:35–45	28
11. Mark 14:1–11	30
12. Mark 14:53–65	32
13. Mark 15:1–20	34
Extra: What is Crucixion?	36
14. Mark 15:33–47	40
15. Mark 16:1–8	42
Conclusion: What Now?	44

INTRODUCTION

THE GOSPEL ACCORDING TO MARK

The Gospel According to Mark is the earliest biography of Jesus. It was written by Mark, a follower of Jesus and leader in the early church, sometime between 55–60 AD, just two decades after Jesus taught, ministered, performed miracles, died on the cross, and rose again.

Mark wrote this book while Jesus' followers and enemies were still alive. If his writing was anything more than the truth, the whole truth, and nothing but the truth, people would have spoken up, Mark's work would have been quickly dismissed, and we wouldn't be reading it thousands of years later.

But Mark's writing *has* stood the test of time (and copies of this book have survived since ancient times, so we don't have to worry that it has been edited.)[1] We can trust it as a historically accurate telling of who Jesus was and what he did.

ONE BIG QUESTION

Mark wrote this entire book to ask one question, "Who is Jesus?" Mark presents a lot of evidence to show you the truth: Jesus is the Son of God. Mark is inviting you to consider all the evidence and make a decision for yourself based on the truth: Mark presents Jesus as the Son of God — who do *you* think Jesus is?

Mark's Gospel is split into three main sections:
- 1:1–8:26 — Jesus' ministry (Evidence about who Jesus is)
- 8:27–10:52 — Jesus traveling to Jerusalem (While he traveled, he taught his disciples who he is and what he was going to do to save them.)
- 11–16 — Jesus in Jerusalem (Where he died and rose again for sinners)

---
[1] For more information about why we can trust Mark's Gospel, read "The Historical Reliability of Mark's Gospel" by Peter J. Williams. Available at bethinking.org/is-the-bible-reliable/mark-reliability

All of the events in Mark's Gospel took place in Israel.

HISTORICAL EVENTS

Jesus isn't another fable —he's a historical figure. He's mentioned by ancient Roman historians such as Tacitus (first century) and Suetonius, chief secretary to the Roman emperor in the second century.

If you're interested in history, here's a timeline to help you get your bearings:

- 347 BC — The philosopher Plato dies in Athens, Greece.
- 323 BC — Alexander the Great dies in Babylon.
- 27 BC — The beginning of the *Pax Romana* in the Roman Empire.
- 5–6 BC — Jesus is born.
- 29 AD — Jesus begins his ministry.
- April 3, 33 AD —Jesus dies on the cross.
- April 5, 33 AD —Jesus rises from the dead.
- 68 AD —The Roman Empire Nero dies.
- 71 AD — The Gladiator Sparticus dies.
- 220 AD —The Han Dynasty in China falls

When you read Mark's Gospel, you can have confidence that you're reading about real events that really happened in a real place. This leaves us with two really important questions: What do these events tell us about who Jesus is? And how will you respond?

HOW TO USE THIS JOURNAL

This book is meant to be read, written in, and, most importantly, believed. It was designed for a Christian and non-Christian to read together, but you can also use it on your own.

There are questions in this journal to help you reflect on the Bible readings. Don't allow these questions to be a distraction (don't just skim the Bible passage looking for the answers) — discipline yourself to read the Bible passage carefully one or two times before answering any of the questions.

If you are a Christian, get an extra copy to give to a non-Christian friend and ask them to work through it with you. Make a plan to meet up regularly (we suggest once a week). When you meet up, go through the book together: read the passage, complete the activities, answer the questions, and pray together.

If you aren't a Christian, curious about Jesus, or not sure where you stand, we're so glad you're reading this. This book is for you! We hope you'll read this book humbly (because Jesus is the king and you aren't) and expectantly (because Jesus really is powerful and able to change your life).

You'll also find suggested prayers at the end of every section. We hope you'll use these prayers as a way to ask Jesus to reveal the truth to you.

ONE MORE NOTE...

After Mark was written, Christians divided it up into chapters and verses to make it easier to reference and read. In this book, you might see numbers like this: Mark 1:1–13.

The first number is the chapter number. All the numbers after the colon are verse numbers. You can find the verses marked in this journal (and in most Bibles) by a little number at the beginning.
Those little numbers look like this: [1].

Not every verse in Mark's Gospel is included in this journal — that's just to make this journal as simple as possible to use, not because we're trying to hide anything. Feel free to grab a Bible and "fill in the gaps."

"For even the Son of Man did not come to be served, but to serve, and to give his life as a ransom for many."

Mark 10:45

MARK 1:1–13

Mark begins his biography of Jesus by talking about John the Baptist, a preacher who "prepared the way" for Jesus. As you read, listen for how everyone in the passage (Mark, John, God) described Jesus.

[1] The beginning of the gospel of Jesus Christ, the Son of God. [2] As it is written in Isaiah the prophet:

> See, I am sending my messenger ahead of you;
> he will prepare your way.
> [3] A voice of one crying out in the wilderness:
> Prepare the way for the Lord;
> make his paths straight!

[4] John came baptizing in the wilderness and proclaiming a baptism of repentance for the forgiveness of sins. [5] The whole Judean countryside and all the people of Jerusalem were going out to him, and they were baptized by him in the Jordan River, confessing their sins. [6] John wore a camel-hair garment with a leather belt around his waist and ate locusts and wild honey.

[7] He proclaimed, "One who is more powerful than I am is coming after me. I am not worthy to stoop down and untie the strap of his sandals. [8] I baptize you with water, but he will baptize you with the Holy Spirit."

[9] In those days Jesus came from Nazareth in Galilee and was baptized in the Jordan by John. [10] As soon as he came up out of the water, he saw the heavens being torn open and the Spirit descending on him like a dove. [11] And a voice came from heaven: "You are my beloved Son; with you I am well-pleased."

[12] Immediately the Spirit drove him into the wilderness. [13] He was in the wilderness forty days, being tempted by Satan. He was with the wild animals, and the angels were serving him.

How did each character in this passage describe Jesus?

Person	How Did They Describe Jesus?
Mark	
John the Baptist	
God	

Do you believe these things about Jesus? Which of these statements about Jesus is the hardest for you to believe?

If these statements about Jesus are true, do you think it would be good news for your life? Why or why not?

What are some things in this passage that point to Jesus' greatness? (For example, see verses 7 and 13). If Jesus really is this great, how should that change the way we relate to him?

KNOW THIS: Jesus is the Son of God — we are unworthy to untie his sandals.
PRAY: Jesus, help me to know and believe the truth about you.

MARK 1:14–28

Mark's Gospel tells us incredible (and true!) stories about how Jesus preached, called followers, and healed the sick. As you read, underline Jesus' words.

[14] After John was arrested, Jesus went to Galilee, proclaiming the good news of God: [15] "The time is fulfilled, and the kingdom of God has come near. **Repent** and believe the good news!"

[16] As he passed alongside the Sea of Galilee, he saw Simon and Andrew, Simon's brother, casting a net into the sea—for they were fishermen. [17] "Follow me," Jesus told them, "and I will make you fish for people." [18] Immediately they left their nets and followed him. [19] Going on a little farther, he saw James the son of Zebedee and his brother John in a boat putting their nets in order. [20] Immediately he called them, and they left their father Zebedee in the boat with the hired men and followed him.

[21] They went into Capernaum, and right away he entered the synagogue on the Sabbath and began to teach. [22] They were astonished at his teaching because he was teaching them as one who had authority, and not like the scribes. [23] Just then a man with an unclean spirit was in their synagogue. He cried out, [24] "What do you have to do with us, Jesus of Nazareth? Have you come to destroy us? I know who you are—the Holy One of God!" [25] Jesus rebuked him saying, "Be silent, and come out of him!" [26] And the unclean spirit threw him into convulsions, shouted with a loud voice, and came out of him.

[27] They were all amazed, and so they began to ask each other, "What is this? A new teaching with authority! He commands even the unclean spirits, and they obey him." [28] At once the news about him spread throughout the entire vicinity of Galilee.

Key Words: "Repent" (1:15) means to turn away from our sins and towards God. When we repent, we acknowledge that we have lived for ourselves or other "kings," and then give ourselves to follow the one true King — Jesus Christ.

Learn more: Acts 3:17–20, 2 Corinthians 7:9–10

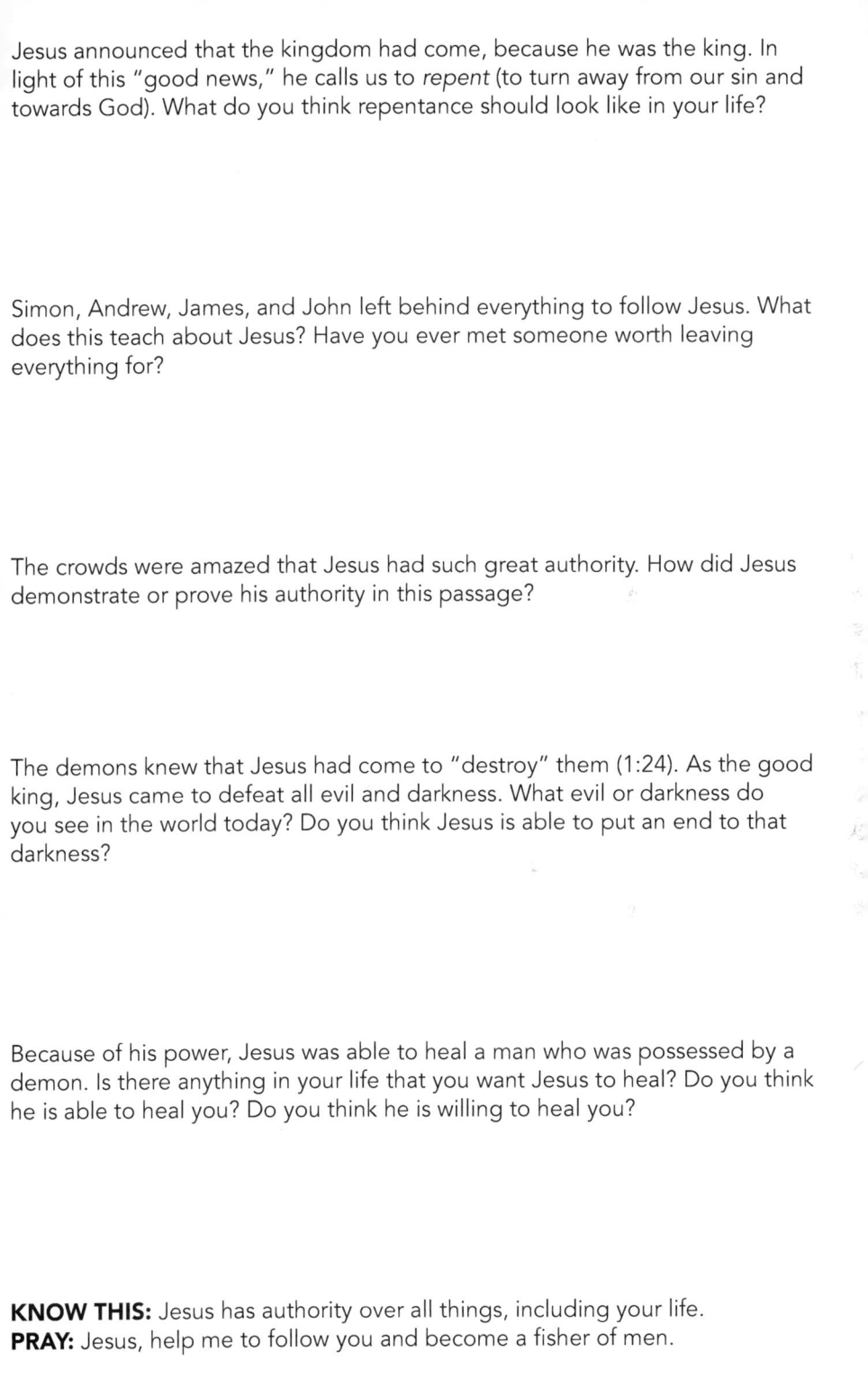

Jesus announced that the kingdom had come, because he was the king. In light of this "good news," he calls us to *repent* (to turn away from our sin and towards God). What do you think repentance should look like in your life?

Simon, Andrew, James, and John left behind everything to follow Jesus. What does this teach about Jesus? Have you ever met someone worth leaving everything for?

The crowds were amazed that Jesus had such great authority. How did Jesus demonstrate or prove his authority in this passage?

The demons knew that Jesus had come to "destroy" them (1:24). As the good king, Jesus came to defeat all evil and darkness. What evil or darkness do you see in the world today? Do you think Jesus is able to put an end to that darkness?

Because of his power, Jesus was able to heal a man who was possessed by a demon. Is there anything in your life that you want Jesus to heal? Do you think he is able to heal you? Do you think he is willing to heal you?

KNOW THIS: Jesus has authority over all things, including your life.
PRAY: Jesus, help me to follow you and become a fisher of men.

MARK 2:1–17

*Today we will read two more stories about Jesus healing.
As you read, underline everything Jesus says about sin and sinners.*

¹ When he entered Capernaum again after some days, it was reported that he was at home. ² So many people gathered together that there was no more room, not even in the doorway, and he was speaking the word to them. ³ They came to him bringing a paralytic, carried by four of them. ⁴ Since they were not able to bring him to Jesus because of the crowd, they removed the roof above him, and after digging through it, they lowered the mat on which the paralytic was lying. ⁵ Seeing their faith, Jesus told the paralytic, "Son, your sins are forgiven." ⁶ But some of the scribes were sitting there, questioning in their hearts: ⁷ "Why does he speak like this? He's blaspheming! Who can forgive sins but God alone?" ⁸ Right away Jesus perceived in his spirit that they were thinking like this within themselves and said to them, "Why are you thinking these things in your hearts? ⁹ Which is easier: to say to the paralytic, 'Your sins are forgiven,' or to say, 'Get up, take your mat, and walk'? ¹⁰ But so that you may know that the Son of Man has authority on earth to forgive sins"—he told the paralytic—¹¹ "I tell you: get up, take your mat, and go home." ¹² Immediately he got up, took the mat, and went out in front of everyone. As a result, they were all astounded and gave glory to God, saying, "We have never seen anything like this!"

¹³ Jesus went out again beside the sea. The whole crowd was coming to him, and he was teaching them. ¹⁴ Then, passing by, he saw Levi the son of Alphaeus sitting at the tax office, and he said to him, "Follow me," and he got up and followed him. ¹⁵ While he was reclining at the table in Levi's house, many tax collectors and sinners were eating with Jesus and his disciples, for there were many who were following him. ¹⁶ When the scribes who were Pharisees saw that he was eating with sinners and tax collectors, they asked his disciples, "Why does he eat with tax collectors and sinners?" ¹⁷ When Jesus heard this, he told them, "It is not those who are well who need a doctor, but those who are sick. I didn't come to call the righteous, but sinners."

The crowds (rightly) pointed out that only God can forgive sins (verse 7). Jesus is able to forgive sins because he *is* the one true God. This is obviously a big claim to make about yourself, but how did Jesus prove it? (See verses 10–12)

Who did Jesus call to follow him in the second story? What did the Pharisees (religious leaders) say about this?

What did Jesus mean when he said, "It is not those who are well who need a doctor, but those who are sick" (verse 17)? Specifically, who is the "physician?" How does he heal?

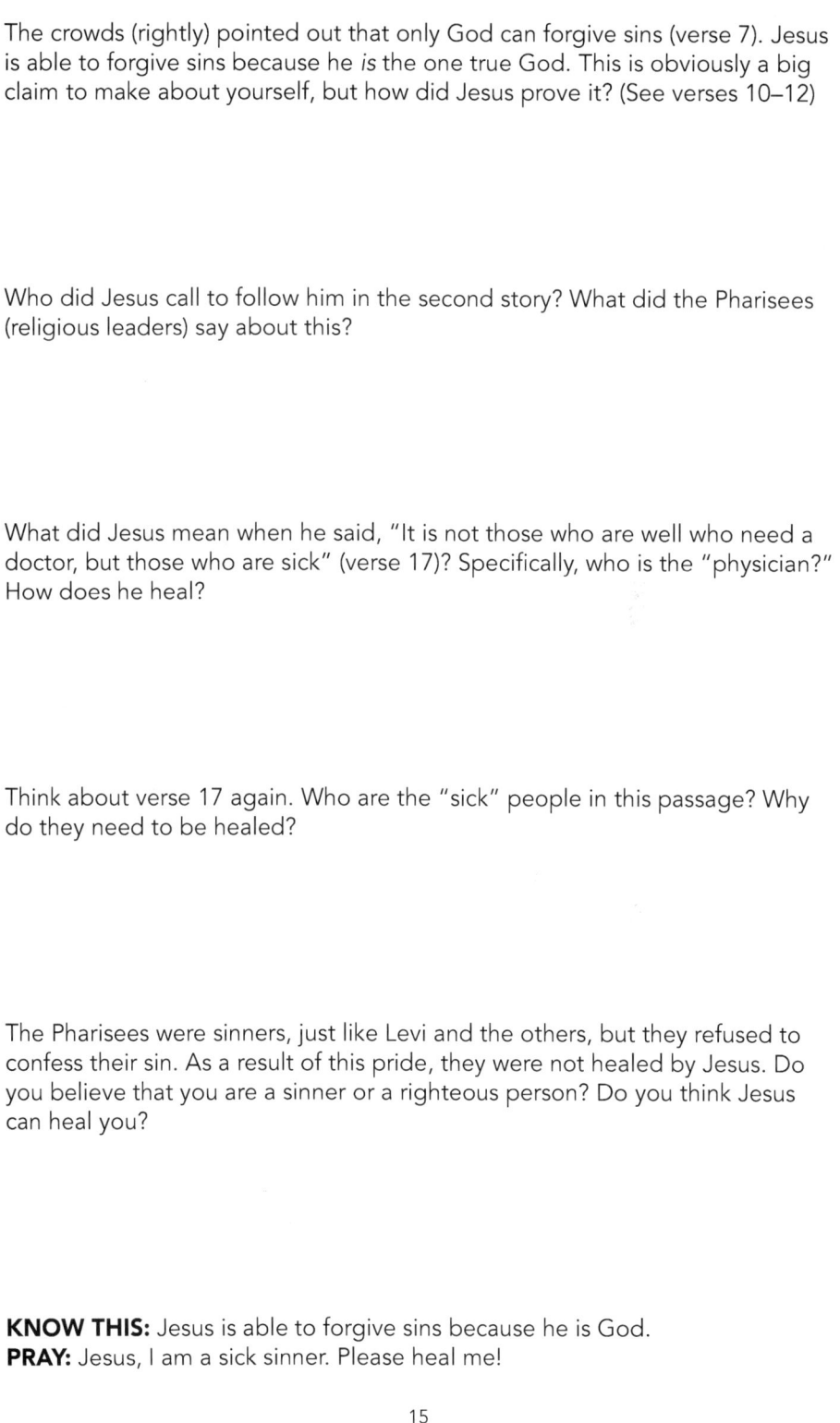

Think about verse 17 again. Who are the "sick" people in this passage? Why do they need to be healed?

The Pharisees were sinners, just like Levi and the others, but they refused to confess their sin. As a result of this pride, they were not healed by Jesus. Do you believe that you are a sinner or a righteous person? Do you think Jesus can heal you?

KNOW THIS: Jesus is able to forgive sins because he is God.
PRAY: Jesus, I am a sick sinner. Please heal me!

MARK 4:35–41

Today we will read about one of Jesus' most famous miracles. As you read, underline all of Jesus' words.

[35] On that day, when evening had come, he told them, "Let's cross over to the other side of the sea." [36] So they left the crowd and took him along since he was in the boat. And other boats were with him. [37] A great windstorm arose, and the waves were breaking over the boat, so that the boat was already being swamped. [38] He was in the stern, sleeping on the cushion. So they woke him up and said to him, "Teacher! Don't you care that we're going to die?"

[39] He got up, rebuked the wind, and said to the sea, "Silence! Be still!" The wind ceased, and there was a great calm. [40] Then he said to them, "Why are you afraid? Do you still have no faith?"

[41] And they were terrified and asked one another, "Who then is this? Even the wind and the sea obey him!"

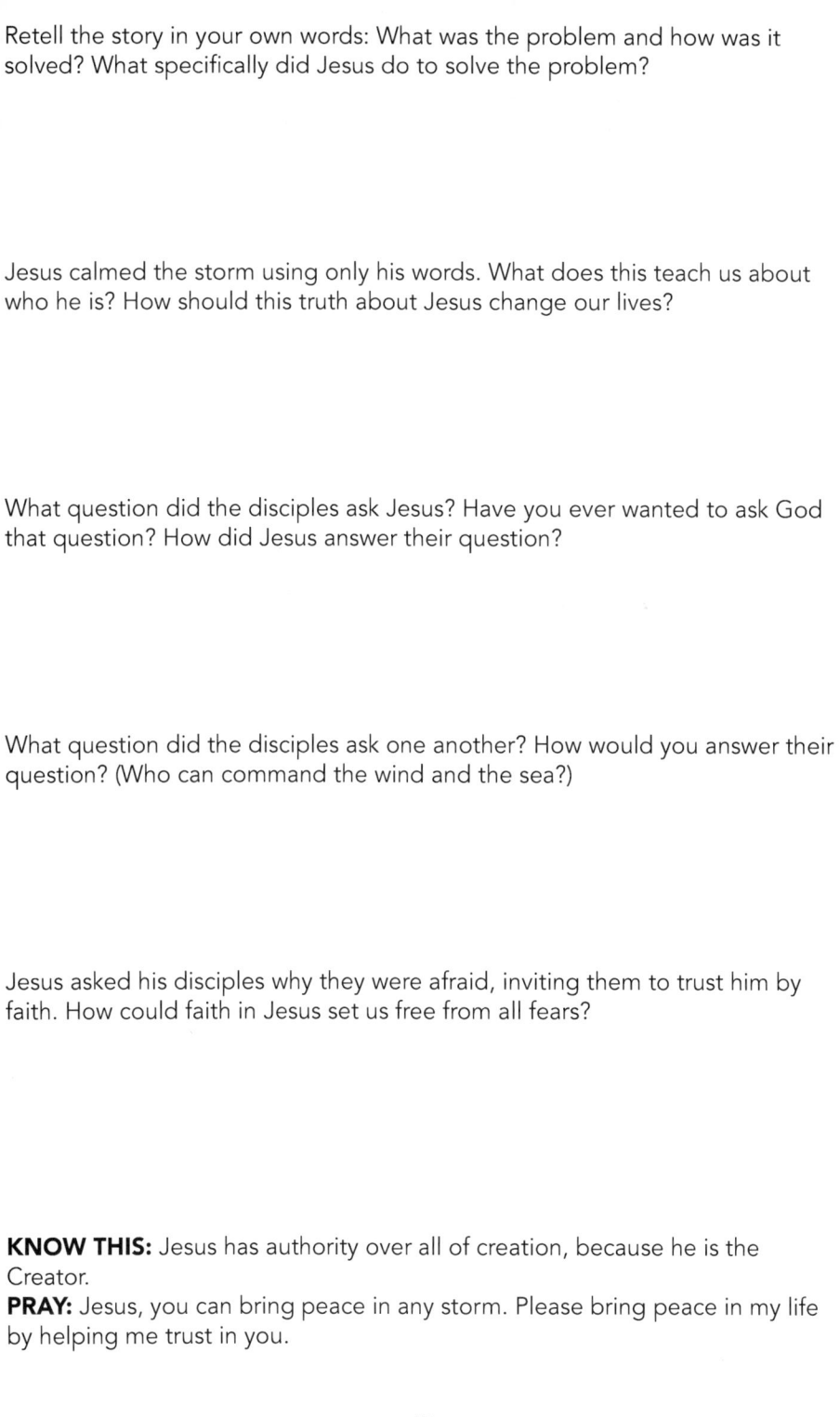

Retell the story in your own words: What was the problem and how was it solved? What specifically did Jesus do to solve the problem?

Jesus calmed the storm using only his words. What does this teach us about who he is? How should this truth about Jesus change our lives?

What question did the disciples ask Jesus? Have you ever wanted to ask God that question? How did Jesus answer their question?

What question did the disciples ask one another? How would you answer their question? (Who can command the wind and the sea?)

Jesus asked his disciples why they were afraid, inviting them to trust him by faith. How could faith in Jesus set us free from all fears?

KNOW THIS: Jesus has authority over all of creation, because he is the Creator.
PRAY: Jesus, you can bring peace in any storm. Please bring peace in my life by helping me trust in you.

MARK 6:30–44

Today we're going to read about another of Jesus' most famous miracles. As you read, circle every word that describes a quantity.

[30] The apostles gathered around Jesus and reported to him all that they had done and taught. [31] He said to them, "Come away by yourselves to a remote place and rest for a while." For many people were coming and going, and they did not even have time to eat.

[32] So they went away in the boat by themselves to a remote place, [33] but many saw them leaving and recognized them, and they ran on foot from all the towns and arrived ahead of them.

[34] When he went ashore, he saw a large crowd and had compassion on them, because they were like sheep without a shepherd. Then he began to teach them many things.

[35] When it grew late, his disciples approached him and said, "This place is deserted, and it is already late. [36] Send them away so that they can go into the surrounding countryside and villages to buy themselves something to eat."

[37] "You give them something to eat," he responded.

They said to him, "Should we go and buy two hundred denarii worth of bread and give them something to eat?"

[38] He asked them, "How many loaves do you have? Go and see."

When they found out they said, "Five, and two fish." [39] Then he instructed them to have all the people sit down in groups on the green grass. [40] So they sat down in groups of hundreds and fifties. [41] He took the five loaves and the two fish, and looking up to heaven, he blessed and broke the loaves. He kept giving them to his disciples to set before the people. He also divided the two fish among them all. [42] Everyone ate and was satisfied. [43] They picked up twelve baskets full of pieces of bread and fish. [44] Now those who had eaten the loaves were five thousand men.

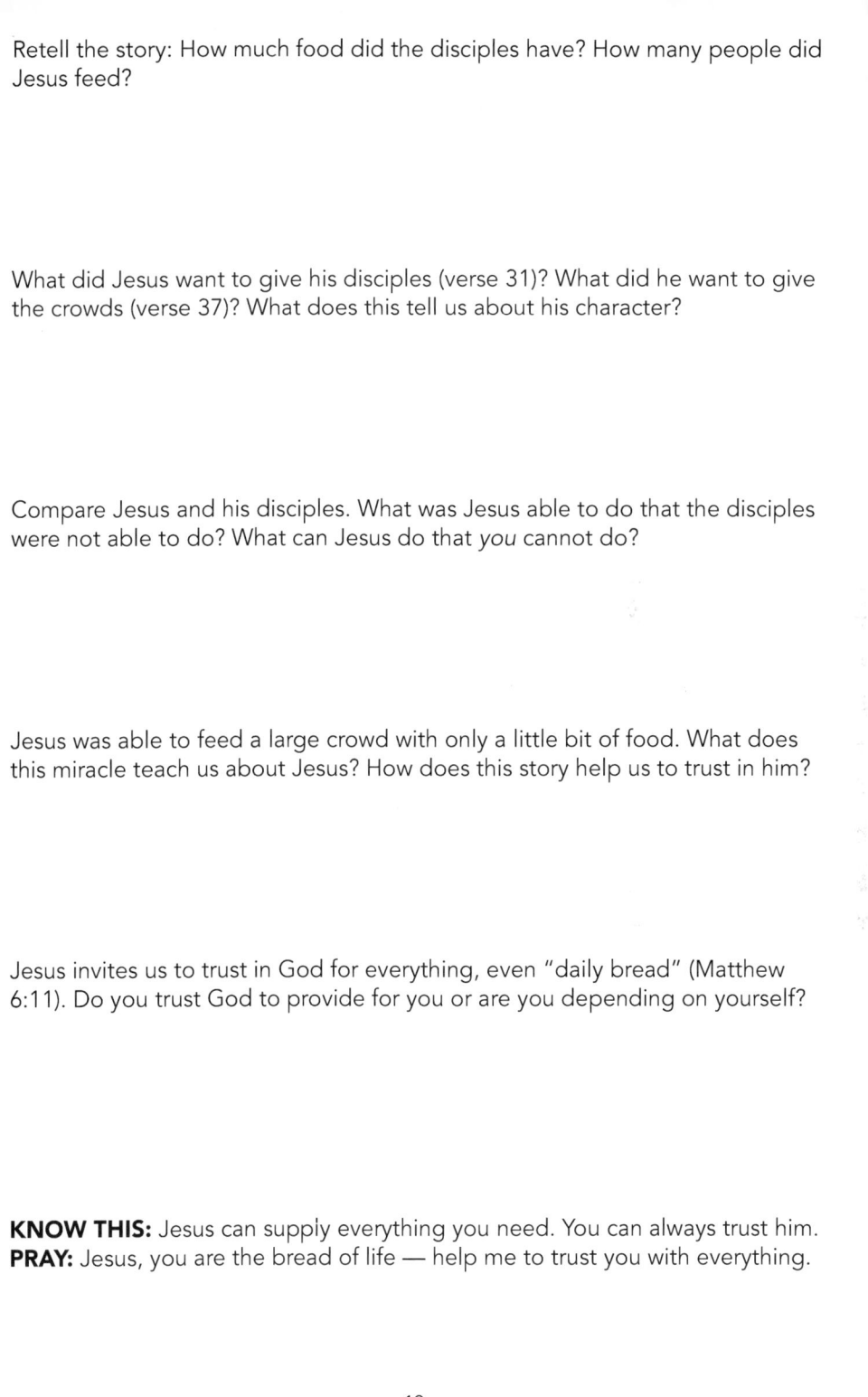

Retell the story: How much food did the disciples have? How many people did Jesus feed?

What did Jesus want to give his disciples (verse 31)? What did he want to give the crowds (verse 37)? What does this tell us about his character?

Compare Jesus and his disciples. What was Jesus able to do that the disciples were not able to do? What can Jesus do that *you* cannot do?

Jesus was able to feed a large crowd with only a little bit of food. What does this miracle teach us about Jesus? How does this story help us to trust in him?

Jesus invites us to trust in God for everything, even "daily bread" (Matthew 6:11). Do you trust God to provide for you or are you depending on yourself?

KNOW THIS: Jesus can supply everything you need. You can always trust him.
PRAY: Jesus, you are the bread of life — help me to trust you with everything.

MARK 6:45–56

Today we're going to read about what happened after Jesus fed the 5,000. As you read, circle every reference to Jesus (including pronouns).

⁴⁵ Immediately he made his disciples get into the boat and go ahead of him to the other side, to Bethsaida, while he dismissed the crowd. ⁴⁶ After he said good-bye to them, he went away to the mountain to pray. ⁴⁷ Well into the night, the boat was in the middle of the sea, and he was alone on the land. ⁴⁸ He saw them straining at the oars, because the wind was against them. Very early in the morning he came toward them walking on the sea and wanted to pass by them. ⁴⁹ When they saw him walking on the sea, they thought it was a ghost and cried out, ⁵⁰ because they all saw him and were terrified. Immediately he spoke with them and said, "Have courage! It is I. Don't be afraid." ⁵¹ Then he got into the boat with them, and the wind ceased. They were completely astounded, ⁵² because they had not understood about the loaves. Instead, their hearts were hardened.

⁵³ When they had crossed over, they came to shore at Gennesaret and anchored there. ⁵⁴ As they got out of the boat, people immediately recognized him. ⁵⁵ They hurried throughout that region and began to carry the sick on mats to wherever they heard he was. ⁵⁶ Wherever he went, into villages, towns, or the country, they laid the sick in the marketplaces and begged him that they might touch just the end of his robe. And everyone who touched it was healed.

What miracles did Jesus perform in this reading? Write a list of them here:

What were the disciples doing before they saw Jesus (see verse 48)?
How did the disciples respond when they saw Jesus walking on the water?

What did Jesus tell the disciples while he was walking on the water?
Why were the disciples afraid? Why did they not need to be afraid?

Read verses 51–52 again. Why were the disciples "completely astounded?" (Look for the word "because.")

What did Jesus reveal about himself when he fed the 5,000 (and again when he walked on the water) that helps us to not be afraid?

Jesus, who was able to feed the 5,000, walk on the water, and calm the storm, is trustworthy. How should can this truth about him change your life?

KNOW THIS: Jesus is mighty. There is nothing he cannot do.
PRAY: Jesus, help me trust in you and not be afraid.

MARK 7:1–15

Today we will read about a conflict that Jesus had with the Pharisees (religious leaders who focused on external purity) about religious traditions. As you read, listen for what was wrong with the Pharisees' religious activity.

[1] The Pharisees and some of the scribes who had come from Jerusalem gathered around him. [2] They observed that some of his disciples were eating bread with unclean—that is, unwashed—hands. [3] (For the Pharisees and all the Jews do not eat unless they give their hands a ceremonial washing, keeping the tradition of the elders. [4] When they come from the marketplace, they do not eat unless they have washed. And there are many other customs they have received and keep, like the washing of cups, pitchers, kettles, and dining couches.) [5] So the Pharisees and the scribes asked him, "Why don't your disciples live according to the tradition of the elders, instead of eating bread with ceremonially unclean hands?"

[6] He answered them, "Isaiah prophesied correctly about you hypocrites, as it is written:

> This people honors me with their lips, but their heart is far from me.
> [7] They worship me in vain, teaching as doctrines human commands.

[8] Abandoning the command of God, you hold on to human tradition." [9] He also said to them, "You have a fine way of invalidating God's command in order to set up your tradition! [10] For Moses said: 'Honor your father and your mother;' and 'Whoever speaks evil of father or mother must be put to death.' [11] But you say, 'If anyone tells his father or mother: Whatever benefit you might have received from me is *corban*'" (that is, an offering devoted to God), [12] "you no longer let him do anything for his father or mother. [13] You nullify the word of God by your tradition that you have handed down. And you do many other similar things."

[14] Summoning the crowd again, he told them, "Listen to me, all of you, and understand: [15] Nothing that goes into a person from outside can defile him but the things that come out of a person are what defile him."

What problem did the Pharisees have with Jesus?

What problem did Jesus have with the Pharisees? What does it mean to honor God with your lips but have a heart that is far from him? (See verses 6–7)

What does Jesus say is more important than "human tradition?" (See verse 8, 9, 13)

Why is the word of God more important than human tradition?

How should we respond to the Bible, since it really is the Word of God (not merely human tradition)?

What do you think it would look like for you to honor God with your lips *and* your heart?

KNOW THIS: Jesus alone has perfectly honored God. We can trust him.
PRAY: Jesus, help me to honor God with my whole heart.

MARK 8:27–38

Today we will read about who Jesus really is and what it means to follow him. As you read, underline everything that Jesus says he will do.

²⁷ Jesus went out with his disciples to the villages of Caesarea Philippi. And on the road he asked his disciples, "Who do people say that I am?"

²⁸ They answered him, "John the Baptist; others, Elijah; still others, one of the prophets."

²⁹ "But you," he asked them, "who do you say that I am?"

Peter answered him, "You are the **Messiah**." ³⁰ And he strictly warned them to tell no one about him.

³¹ Then he began to teach them that it was necessary for the Son of Man to suffer many things and be rejected by the elders, chief priests, and scribes, be killed, and rise after three days. ³² He spoke openly about this. Peter took him aside and began to rebuke him. ³³ But turning around and looking at his disciples, he rebuked Peter and said, "Get behind me, Satan! You are not thinking about God's concerns but human concerns."

³⁴ Calling the crowd along with his disciples, he said to them, "If anyone wants to follow after me, let him deny himself, take up his cross, and follow me. ³⁵ For whoever wants to save his life will lose it, but whoever loses his life because of me and the gospel will save it. ³⁶ For what does it benefit someone to gain the whole world and yet lose his life? ³⁷ What can anyone give in exchange for his life? ³⁸ For whoever is ashamed of me and my words in this adulterous and sinful generation, the Son of Man will also be ashamed of him when he comes in the glory of his Father with the holy angels."

Key Words: "Messiah" (8:29) means "anointed one." In the Old Testament, the Messiah was a great hero who would be anointed by God to rule as the King of Israel and all of the world. Jesus is that great king.

Learn more: Psalm 2, Daniel 7, John 1:35–51

What are some things that this passages teaches us about Jesus? Make a list:

After Peter correctly identifies Jesus as the Messiah, the King, Jesus described what he would do. What did Jesus say he was going to do?

Peter was shocked by Jesus' description of his life in verse 31. Why is this a surprising way for a king to live?

Jesus says all of his sufferings and death were "necessary" (verse 31) and when Peter said that Jesus did not have to die, Jesus rebuked him (verse 33). Why was it necessary for Jesus to die?

Jesus calls his disciples to also lay down thier lives in order to truly live. What does it look like for you to deny yourself and follow Jesus?

KNOW THIS: Jesus is the Messiah — the King who gave himself so that rebels might live.
PRAY: Jesus, you took up your cross to save me. Help me to take up my cross to follow you.

MARK 10:17–31

Today we're going to read Jesus' teaching about entering his Kingdom. As we read, draw a star next to everything that Jesus said.

[17] As he was setting out on a journey, a man ran up, knelt down before him, and asked him, "Good teacher, what must I do to inherit eternal life?"

[18] "Why do you call me good?" Jesus asked him. "No one is good except God alone. [19] You know the commandments: Do not murder; do not commit adultery; do not steal; do not bear false witness; do not defraud; honor your father and mother."

[20] He said to him, "Teacher, I have kept all these from my youth."

[21] Looking at him, Jesus loved him and said to him, "You lack one thing: Go, sell all you have and give to the poor, and you will have treasure in heaven. Then come, follow me." [22] But he was dismayed by this demand, and he went away grieving, because he had many possessions.

[23] Jesus looked around and said to his disciples, "How hard it is for those who have wealth to enter the kingdom of God!"

[24] The disciples were astonished at his words. Again Jesus said to them, "Children, how hard it is to enter the kingdom of God! [25] It is easier for a camel to go through the eye of a needle than for a rich person to enter the kingdom of God." [26] They were even more astonished, saying to one another, "Then who can be saved?"

[27] Looking at them, Jesus said, "With man it is impossible, but not with God, because all things are possible with God."

[28] Peter began to tell him, "Look, we have left everything and followed you."

[29] "Truly I tell you," Jesus said, "there is no one who has left house or brothers or sisters or mother or father or children or fields for my sake and for the sake of the gospel, [30] who will not receive a hundred times more, now at this time—houses, brothers and sisters, mothers and children, and fields, with persecutions—and eternal life in the age to come. [31] But many who are first will be last, and the last first."

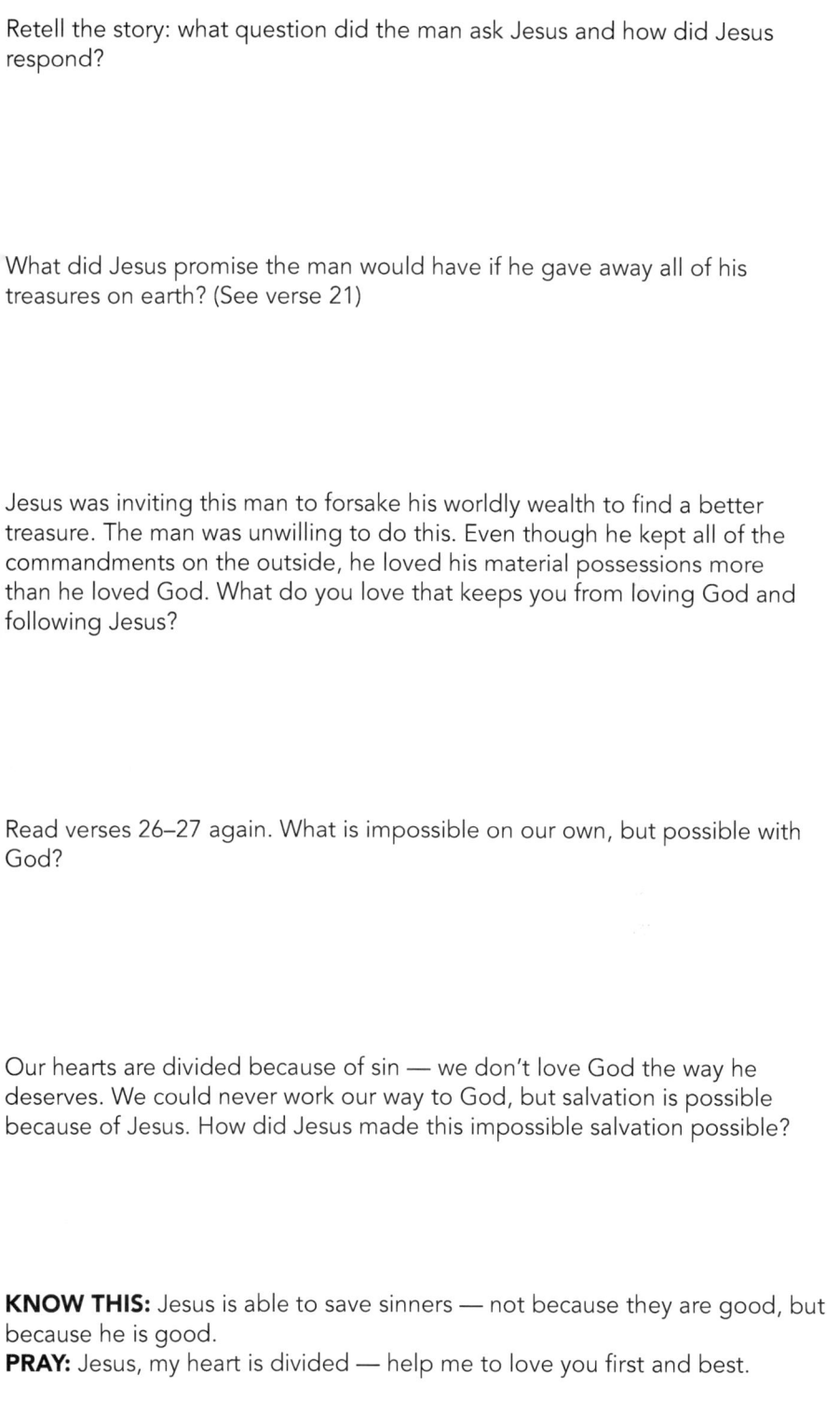

Retell the story: what question did the man ask Jesus and how did Jesus respond?

What did Jesus promise the man would have if he gave away all of his treasures on earth? (See verse 21)

Jesus was inviting this man to forsake his worldly wealth to find a better treasure. The man was unwilling to do this. Even though he kept all of the commandments on the outside, he loved his material possessions more than he loved God. What do you love that keeps you from loving God and following Jesus?

Read verses 26–27 again. What is impossible on our own, but possible with God?

Our hearts are divided because of sin — we don't love God the way he deserves. We could never work our way to God, but salvation is possible because of Jesus. How did Jesus made this impossible salvation possible?

KNOW THIS: Jesus is able to save sinners — not because they are good, but because he is good.
PRAY: Jesus, my heart is divided — help me to love you first and best.

MARK 10:35–45

Today we're going to read an interesting conversation that Jesus had with his disciples. As you read, underline everything that Jesus said he was going to do.

35 James and John, the sons of Zebedee, approached him and said, "Teacher, we want you to do whatever we ask you."

36 "What do you want me to do for you?" he asked them.

37 They answered him, "Allow us to sit at your right and at your left in your glory."

38 Jesus said to them, "You don't know what you're asking. Are you able to drink the cup I drink or to be baptized with the baptism I am baptized with?"

39 "We are able," they told him.

Jesus said to them, "You will drink the cup I drink, and you will be baptized with the baptism I am baptized with. 40 But to sit at my right or left is not mine to give; instead, it is for those for whom it has been prepared."

41 When the ten disciples heard this, they began to be indignant with James and John. 42 Jesus called them over and said to them, "You know that those who are regarded as rulers of the Gentiles lord it over them, and those in high positions act as tyrants over them. 43 But it is not so among you. On the contrary, whoever wants to become great among you will be your servant, 44 and whoever wants to be first among you will be a slave to all. 45 For even the **Son of Man** did not come to be served, but to serve, and to give his life as a ransom for many."

Key Words: "Son of Man" (10:45) is a figure from the Old Testament who was equal with God. God's people were expecting this Son to come and receive great authority to rule as the king of all nations forever.

Learn more: Daniel 7:13–14, Matthew 16:13–28

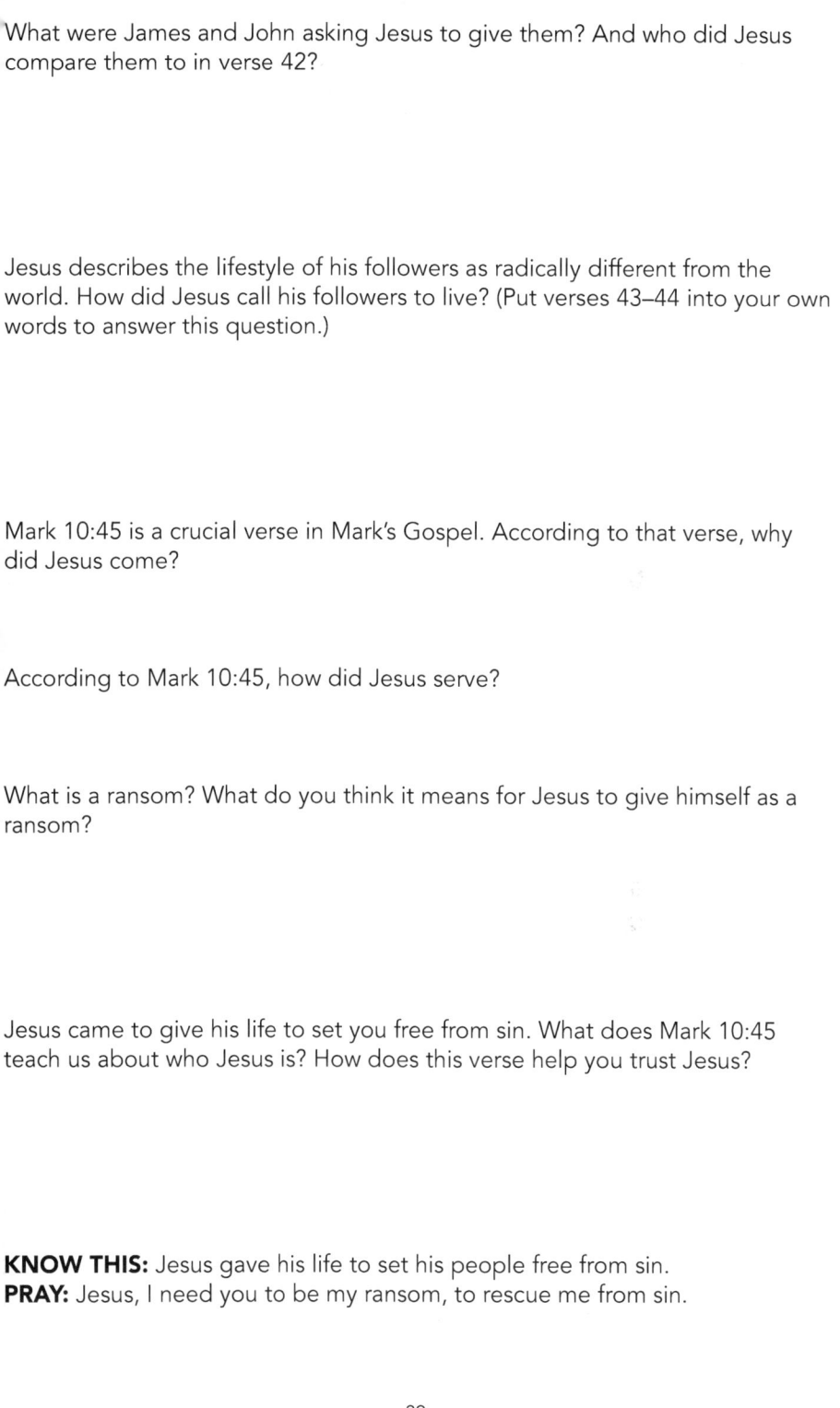

What were James and John asking Jesus to give them? And who did Jesus compare them to in verse 42?

Jesus describes the lifestyle of his followers as radically different from the world. How did Jesus call his followers to live? (Put verses 43–44 into your own words to answer this question.)

Mark 10:45 is a crucial verse in Mark's Gospel. According to that verse, why did Jesus come?

According to Mark 10:45, how did Jesus serve?

What is a ransom? What do you think it means for Jesus to give himself as a ransom?

Jesus came to give his life to set you free from sin. What does Mark 10:45 teach us about who Jesus is? How does this verse help you trust Jesus?

KNOW THIS: Jesus gave his life to set his people free from sin.
PRAY: Jesus, I need you to be my ransom, to rescue me from sin.

MARK 14:1–11

Today, we're going to read about an interaction that Jesus had with a woman in Jerusalem. As you read, circle every reference to Jesus (including pronouns).

¹ It was two days before the **Passover** and the Festival of Unleavened Bread. The chief priests and the scribes were looking for a cunning way to arrest Jesus and kill him. ² "Not during the festival," they said, "so that there won't be a riot among the people."

³ While he was in Bethany at the house of Simon the leper, as he was reclining at the table, a woman came with an alabaster jar of very expensive perfume of pure nard. She broke the jar and poured it on his head. ⁴ But some were expressing indignation to one another: "Why has this perfume been wasted? ⁵ For this perfume might have been sold for more than three hundred denarii and given to the poor." And they began to scold her.

⁶ Jesus replied, "Leave her alone. Why are you bothering her? She has done a noble thing for me. ⁷ You always have the poor with you, and you can do what is good for them whenever you want, but you do not always have me. ⁸ She has done what she could; she has anointed my body in advance for burial. ⁹ Truly I tell you, wherever the gospel is proclaimed in the whole world, what she has done will also be told in memory of her."

¹⁰ Then Judas Iscariot, one of the Twelve, went to the chief priests to betray Jesus to them. ¹¹ And when they heard this, they were glad and promised to give him money. So he started looking for a good opportunity to betray him.

Key Words: "Passover" (14:1) is a Holy Day for the Jewish people, commemorating the Exodus, when God saved them from slavery in Egypt through Moses. When God punished the Egyptians, the Israelites were spared because they sacrificed a lamb to die in their place. Because of the lamb, God's wrath "passed over" them.
Jesus is the Lamb of God; like the Passover Lamb, he was sacrificed in our place so that we can be spared from the wrath of God.

Learn more: Exodus 11–12, 1 Corinthians 5:6–8

What did the woman do for Jesus? Why were some people angry about this?

Jesus defended this woman. Why was her offering a good thing?

What does this story teach us about who Jesus is?

Even though this story is a clear picture of Jesus' greatness, it was also a picture of his coming death. Can you find three ways this passage points us forward to the cross of Christ, where Jesus died for sinners?

1.

2.

3.

Why does Jesus' death make him worthy of all of our worship?

KNOW THIS: Jesus is the Savior who is worthy of all worship.
PRAY: Jesus, you are worthy of all worship because you died to save me. Help me to give all of myself to you.

MARK 14:53–65

Betrayed by his friends and abandoned by many of his followers, Jesus is arrested and led away for an unfair trial. As you read, listen for what charge Jesus' opponents raised against him.

⁵³ They led Jesus away to the high priest, and all the chief priests, the elders, and the scribes assembled. ⁵⁴ Peter followed him at a distance, right into the high priest's courtyard. He was sitting with the servants, warming himself by the fire.

⁵⁵ The chief priests and the whole **Sanhedrin** were looking for testimony against Jesus to put him to death, but they could not find any. ⁵⁶ For many were giving false testimony against him, and the testimonies did not agree. ⁵⁷ Some stood up and gave false testimony against him, stating, ⁵⁸ "We heard him say, 'I will destroy this temple made with human hands, and in three days I will build another not made by hands.'" ⁵⁹ Yet their testimony did not agree even on this.

⁶⁰ Then the high priest stood up before them all and questioned Jesus, "Don't you have an answer to what these men are testifying against you?" ⁶¹ But he kept silent and did not answer. Again the high priest questioned him, "Are you the Messiah, the Son of the Blessed One?"

⁶² "I am," said Jesus, "and you will see the Son of Man seated at the right hand of Power and coming with the clouds of heaven."

⁶³ Then the high priest tore his robes and said, "Why do we still need witnesses? ⁶⁴ You have heard the blasphemy. What is your decision?" They all condemned him as deserving death.

⁶⁵ Then some began to spit on him, to blindfold him, and to beat him, saying, "Prophesy!" The temple servants also took him and slapped him.

Key Words: The **"Sanhedrin"** (14:55) was the Jewish Supreme Court in Jesus' day.

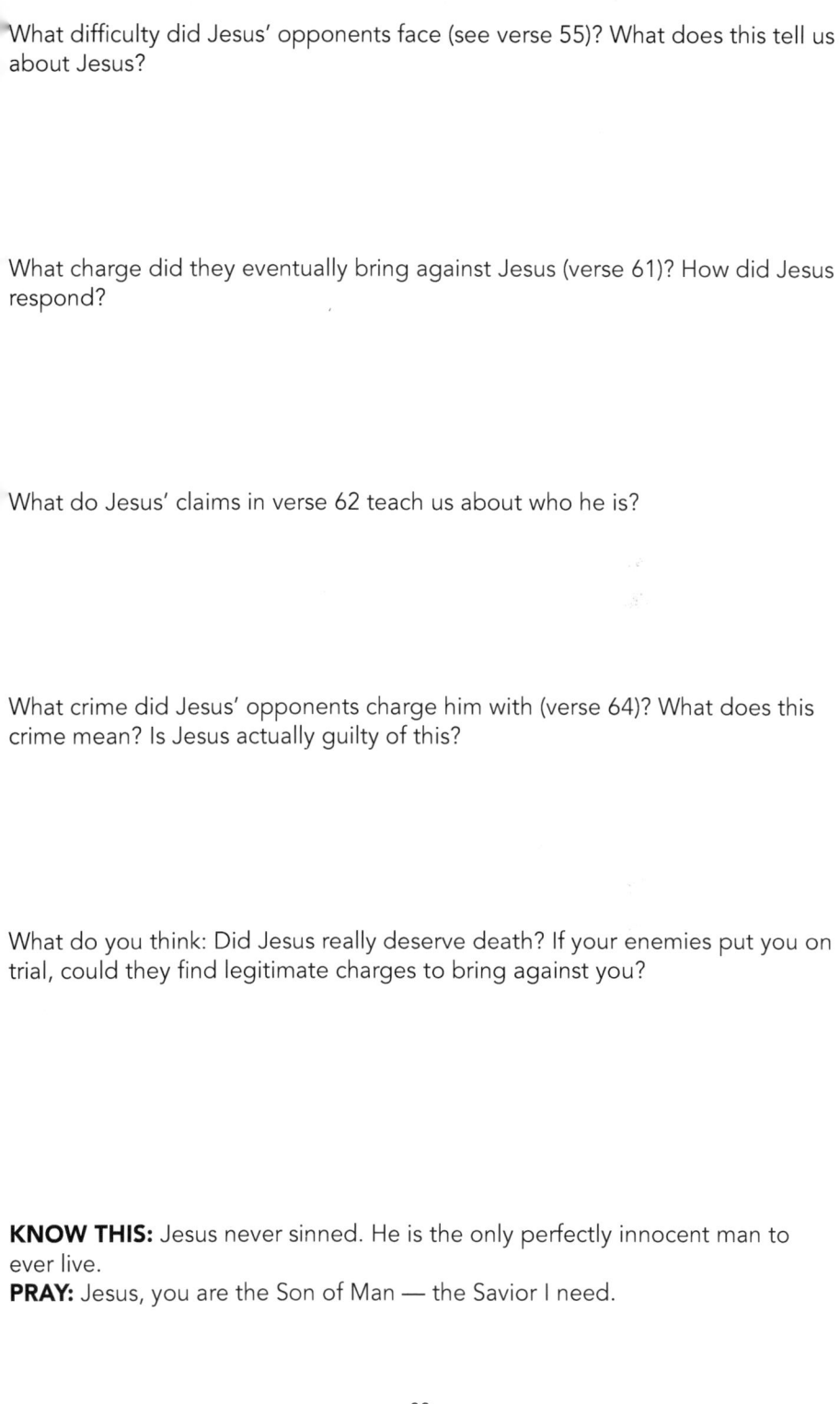

What difficulty did Jesus' opponents face (see verse 55)? What does this tell us about Jesus?

What charge did they eventually bring against Jesus (verse 61)? How did Jesus respond?

What do Jesus' claims in verse 62 teach us about who he is?

What crime did Jesus' opponents charge him with (verse 64)? What does this crime mean? Is Jesus actually guilty of this?

What do you think: Did Jesus really deserve death? If your enemies put you on trial, could they find legitimate charges to bring against you?

KNOW THIS: Jesus never sinned. He is the only perfectly innocent man to ever live.
PRAY: Jesus, you are the Son of Man — the Savior I need.

MARK 15:1–20

*Today we will read about Jesus' interactions with Pilate.
As you read, underline any references to charges against Jesus.*

¹ And as soon as it was morning, the chief priests held a consultation with the elders and scribes and the whole council. And they bound Jesus and led him away and delivered him over to Pilate. ² And Pilate asked him, "Are you the King of the Jews?" And he answered him, "You have said so." ³ And the chief priests accused him of many things. ⁴ And Pilate again asked him, "Have you no answer to make? See how many charges they bring against you." ⁵ But Jesus made no further answer, so that Pilate was amazed.

⁶ At the festival Pilate used to release for the people a prisoner whom they requested. ⁷ There was one named Barabbas, who was in prison with rebels who had committed murder during the rebellion. ⁸ The crowd came up and began to ask Pilate to do for them as was his custom. ⁹ Pilate answered them, "Do you want me to release the king of the Jews for you?" ¹⁰ For he knew it was because of envy that the chief priests had handed him over. ¹¹ But the chief priests stirred up the crowd so that he would release Barabbas to them instead. ¹² Pilate asked them again, "Then what do you want me to do with the one you call the king of the Jews?"

¹³ Again they shouted, "Crucify him!"

¹⁴ Pilate said to them, "Why? What has he done wrong?" But they shouted all the more, "Crucify him!"

¹⁵ Wanting to satisfy the crowd, Pilate released Barabbas to them; and after having Jesus flogged, he handed him over to be crucified. ¹⁶ The soldiers led him away into the palace (that is, the governor's residence) and called the whole company together. ¹⁷ They dressed him in a purple robe, twisted together a crown of thorns, and put it on him. ¹⁸ And they began to salute him, "Hail, king of the Jews!" ¹⁹ They were hitting him on the head with a stick and spitting on him. Getting down on their knees, they were paying him homage. ²⁰ After they had mocked him, they stripped him of the purple robe and put his clothes on him.

How did Jesus respond to Pilate? What does this tell us about Jesus?

What are some of the ways that Jesus suffered in this passage? Make a list here:

Jesus could have prevented this suffering if he had defended himself before Pilate. Why do you think he chose to *not* defend himself?

The soldiers mocked Jesus, dressing him up and saluting him as a king. Why is this an ironic scene?

The innocent Jesus was condemned while an actual criminal, Barabbas, was released. How is this a picture of salvation?

KNOW THIS: Jesus' death was brutally painful, and it was his own plan. He endured the worst death to save us.
PRAY: Jesus, you suffered to save me. Thank you.

WHAT IS CRUCIFIXION?

"THE MOST WRETCHED OF DEATHS"

The Romans were experts at torture. They created and perfected the weapon of crucifixion as a way to ensure none of their enemies could die quickly, but suffer a long, excruciating, public death instead.

Ancient sources tell us that crucifixion was seen as the most horrific way to die (worse than decapitation or being burned alive), which is why the Jewish historian Josephus called it "the most wretched of deaths" (c. 75 AD).

Here's what took place when someone was crucified:

- When a criminal was condemned to be crucified, they were brutally beaten, whipped, and scourged. They were brought within an inch of their lives before even seeing the cross. The torture sometimes included the impaling of the victim's genitals.

- Victims of crucifixion were stripped naked and publicly humiliated as they bled, suffered, and died.

- Victims were forced to stretch out their arms to be physically bound to the cross. After being bound, they were nailed to the cross with thick iron nails driven right through their wrists. The victim's feet were either nailed or bound as well.

- When the cross was raised, victims were hung about 9–12 feet above the ground.

- The crucifixion was public by design — victims were displayed and mocked as they suffered, because the executioners wanted to display thier enemies as less-than-human monsters in their last moments.

- Victims hung on the cross for hours before finally dying, usually by asphyxiation (suffocating under the weight of their own bodies).

DID THIS REALLY HAPPEN TO JESUS?

Today, many people claim that Jesus did not really die on the cross, alledging that the crucifixion was merely a fable or a farse.

However, the earliest sources all agree that Jesus of Nazareth died by crucifixion. This includes the four Gospels, including Mark (see page 6–7 for reasons to trust Mark's historical record of Jesus' life and death), as well as Roman (non-Christian) historians.

One Roman historian, Tacitus, writting around 116 AD, referenced the death of Jesus in great detail. Read this passage and make note of how it confirms the biblical accounts of Jesus' crucifixion:

> **Christus**, from whom the name [Christian] had its origin, **suffered the extreme penalty** during the reign of Tiberius at the hands of one of our procurators, **Pontius Pilatus**, and a most mischievous superstition, thus checked for the moment, again broke out not only in Judæa, the first source of the evil, but even in Rome, where all things hideous and shameful from every part of the world find their centre and become popular.

The death of Jesus has become an accepted fact among historians. Jesus Christ really did die an excruciating, humiliating, degrading death by crucifixion in Jerusalem.

WHY DID JESUS HAVE TO DIE?

Peter, a disciple of Jesus and leader in the early church, said that Jesus' crucifixion was "according to God's determined plan and foreknowledge" (Acts 2:23). Why would God plan the brutal destruction of his own Son? So that he could be raised from the dead, "ending the pains of death" forever for anyone who believes in him (Acts 2:24).

Jesus died to set us free from death.

The Bible teaches that "the wages of sin is death" (Romans 6:23). When Jesus died on the cross, he was not just suffering a horrific punishment at the hands of the Romans, he was also enduring the full wrath of God, which we rightly deserve for our sins.

All of humanity has been held captive by sin. We have sinned against an infinite God and deserve nothing less than an infinite punishment — eternal death.

Jesus came to set the captives free, to release us from the punishment for our sins by paying our debt. Jesus, the sinless one, died for our sins. He took all of our sin onto his record and took all of the punishment onto himself; the infinite God suffered in our place.

This is why Jesus said in Mark 10:45, "the Son of Man did not come to be served, but to serve, and to *give his life as a **ransom for many**.*" We were held captive by our sin, and Jesus came to pay our ransom and set us free. We had earned an infinite punishment, and Jesus took it onto himself.

The one man (Jesus) gave his life "for many." Because he is the eternal God, his death is able to cover the sins of *many*, so that anyone who trusts in Jesus can be confident that their sins have been paid for, the right wrath of God has been assuaged, and we, who once were God's sinful enemies, can be his friends through faith in Christ alone.

"Yet the LORD was pleased to crush him severely.
When you make him a guilt offering,
he will see his seed, he will prolong his days,
and by his hand, the LORD's pleasure will be accomplished.

After his anguish, he will see light and be satisfied.
By his knowledge, my righteous servant will justify many,
and he will carry their iniquities.

Therefore I will give him the many as a portion,
and he will receive the mighty as spoil,
because he willingly submitted to death,
and was counted among the rebels;
yet he bore the sin of many
and interceded for the rebels."

Isaiah 53:10–12
A Prophecy About the Death of Christ

MARK 15:33–47

Today we will read about the death of Jesus.
As you read, underline what the centurion says about Jesus.

[33] And when the sixth hour had come, there was darkness over the whole land until the ninth hour. [34] And at the ninth hour Jesus cried with a loud voice, "*Eloi, Eloi, lema sabachthani?*" which means, "My God, my God, why have you forsaken me?" [35] And some of the bystanders hearing it said, "Behold, he is calling Elijah." [36] And someone ran and filled a sponge with sour wine, put it on a reed and gave it to him to drink, saying, "Wait, let us see whether Elijah will come to take him down." [37] And Jesus uttered a loud cry and breathed his last. [38] And the curtain of the temple was torn in two, from top to bottom. [39] And when the centurion, who stood facing him, saw that in this way he breathed his last, he said, "Truly this man was the Son of God!"

[40] There were also women looking on from a distance, among whom were Mary Magdalene, and Mary the mother of James the younger and of Joses, and Salome. [41] When he was in Galilee, they followed him and ministered to him, and there were also many other women who came up with him to Jerusalem.

[42] And when evening had come, since it was the day of Preparation, that is, the day before the Sabbath, [43] Joseph of Arimathea, a respected member of the council, who was also himself looking for the kingdom of God, took courage and went to Pilate and asked for the body of Jesus. [44] Pilate was surprised to hear that he should have already died. And summoning the centurion, he asked him whether he was already dead. [45] And when he learned from the centurion that he was dead, he granted the corpse to Joseph. [46] And Joseph bought a linen shroud, and taking him down, wrapped him in the linen shroud and laid him in a tomb that had been cut out of the rock. And he rolled a stone against the entrance of the tomb. [47] Mary Magdalene and Mary the mother of Joses saw where he was laid.

Make a list of everyone who saw Jesus' body after he died.

What did Jesus pray before he died? What does this prayer mean?

After Jesus died, "the curtain of the temple was torn in two, from top to bottom." This curtain kept people out of the "Most Holy Place," where God's presence dwelled. Jesus was forsaken and now we can come in to dwell close to God. What does this teach us about God?

Read verse 39 again. What specifically convinced the centurion to believe that Jesus was the Son of God? Why do you think that convinced him?

Like the centurion, you have witnessed the crucifixion of Jesus. What do you believe about who Jesus is? Why did Jesus die?

KNOW THIS: Jesus died to bring you back to God.
PRAY: Jesus, help me believe that you died in my place.

MARK 16:1–8

Today we'll read the ending of Mark's Gospel, which describes Jesus' resurrection from the dead and the (very surprising) reaction of his followers.

¹ When the Sabbath was past, Mary Magdalene, Mary the mother of James, and Salome bought spices, so that they might go and anoint him. ² And very early on the first day of the week, when the sun had risen, they went to the tomb. ³ And they were saying to one another, "Who will roll away the stone for us from the entrance of the tomb?" ⁴ And looking up, they saw that the stone had been rolled back—it was very large. ⁵ And entering the tomb, they saw a young man sitting on the right side, dressed in a white robe, and they were alarmed. ⁶ And he said to them, "Do not be alarmed. You seek Jesus of Nazareth, who was crucified. He has risen; he is not here. See the place where they laid him. ⁷ But go, tell his disciples and Peter that he is going before you to Galilee. There you will see him, just as he told you." ⁸ And they went out and fled from the tomb, for trembling and astonishment had seized them, and they said nothing to anyone, for they were afraid.

Who was going to Jesus' tomb in this story? Why were they going there?

Women, who were often overlooked in the first-century, were the first witnesses to Jesus' resurrection. Why is that significant?

The "young man" at the tomb stated several facts about Jesus. What were they?

Do you believe this young man? Which of the historical facts you listed above do you believe or doubt? Why?

Jesus really did rise from the dead. What does this teach us about who he is?

Next: Turn the page and read "What Now?"

WHAT NOW?

After Jesus rose from the dead, many of his followers saw him, including a crowd of over 500 people at one time (see 1 Corinthians 15:1–8). But Mark's Gospel doesn't mention any of that. Mark abruptly ends his biography about Jesus with mere *reports* about the resurrection, rather than eyewitnesses.

Why did Mark end his gospel so abruptly?

Mark wrote his Gospel to answer one big question: "Who is Jesus?" And he ends his Gospel on a cliff-hanger, eagerly awaiting your response.

In light of all this evidence, who do *you* think Jesus is?

There are really only two possible responses to that question: to believe that Jesus *is* the Son of God or to believe that he is *not* the Son of God.

BELIEVE IN JESUS, THE SON OF GOD...

If Jesus isn't the Son of God, he's probably dead and buried somewhere in Israel. (He can't merely be a good teacher, since his entire message was based on his claim to be God. If that's not true, we can't trust him on anything.)

But what if he really is the Son of God?
- If Jesus is the Son of God, he has authority over everything on earth.
- If Jesus is the Son of God, he has authority over every spirit.
- If Jesus is the Son of God, he is the King of heaven.
- If Jesus is the Son of God, he has authority over you.
- If Jesus is the Son of God, he is able to forgive sins.
- If Jesus is the Son of God, his death on the cross was for you.
- If Jesus is the Son of God, he really did rise from the dead.
- If Jesus is the Son of God, you can be saved from sin by trusting him.
- If Jesus is the Son of God, you can live with God through him.

Jesus *is* the Son of God. He really did rise from the dead. And he really is inviting you to come to him in faith and be saved.

So, in light of all the evidence in Mark's Gospel... who is Jesus? Will you follow him now?

YOUR FIRST STEPS AS A FOLLOWER OF JESUS

If you believe that Jesus really is the Son of God, your next step is to follow him.

Here are some first steps you must take as a follower of Jesus:

- **Trust in Christ alone.** Christianity doesn't start with fixing yourself, it starts by realizing that our good deeds will never be good enough.

- **Repent of your sins.** Turn away from your sins and towards God. Start submitting to God as your king, rather than yourself or anyone else.

- **Join a Christ-following church near you.** Find a church near you that preaches the Bible and will help you follow Jesus. Good books and videos are great, but they will never replace the church. If you live in Washington, DC, please visit us at Pillar Church. You can learn more at PillarDC.com.

- **Get baptized.** Jesus gave water baptism as a special sign to mark our conversion and the salvation that he purchased for us. This happens in a local church.

- **Make disciples.** Jesus calls all of his disciples to be "fishers of men;" to share our story with others, to tell our friends, family, co-workers, and neighbors about how they can be saved from sin. You can start making disciples today!

This resource was created by
Pillar Church of Washington DC.

Our mission is to help people know Jesus and make him known in DC and around the world.

If you are looking for a church family, we hope you'll join us on a Sunday morning.

Learn more at PillarDC.com

THE PRAETORIAN PROJECT

Pillar Church of Washington DC is a part of the **Praetorian Project**, a family of multiplying churches planted near major U.S. military installations worldwide.

Our goal is to reach military servicemembers, civilians, and their families and send them to make disciples wherever their military service brings them.

To learn more about the work of the Project or find a Pillar Church near you, visit PraetorianProject.org

NOTES

Made in United States
Orlando, FL
27 September 2022